SOCI

HOW TO USE SOCIAL MEDIA MARKETING TO GROW YOUR BUSINESS

CONTENTS

INTRODUCTION

The modern Marketing game has changed. In todays world, there are more than 2.3 billion active Social Media users around the globe. The audience of Facebook, Instagram and Snapchat has surpassed traditional media such as television and radio. According to Brandwatch research for 2016, 1 million new active mobile social users are added every day, at an average of one every 12 seconds. It is without a doubt that Social Media Marketing is the future of business engagement. And the future has arrived together with a flashy Snapchat filter.

While digital marketing is well on the way to surpassing traditional marketing, social media is taking it to the next level. As society continues to evolve and become more digital and interconnected on varying platforms, it is essential that your brand is represented in the social media sphere.

This book will discuss the implications of Social Media Marketing on traditional media as well as on businesses themselves. You'll get a closer look at many different Social Media channels. We'll be including their advantages and disadvantages and outlining their unique properties to brands. Successful viral campaigns will be dissected so you can understand how to create viral content. Metrics and Search Engine Optimization will be discussed and outlined, and a breakdown of how to create your Social Media Strategy will follow.

PART 1

OVERVIEW AND GENERAL

CHAPTER 1

WHAT IS SOCIAL MEDIA?

Humans have been social creatures since we descended from the trees and learned to walk. It is in our intrinsic need to communicate and share with one another. This inherent need has manifested itself digitally in the form of social media.

The official definition of Social Media is relatively broad. Merriam-Webster defined it as:

"forms of electronic communication (such as Web sites) through which people create online communities to share information, ideas, personal messages, etc."

You can see how this is a catch-all definition that encompasses messaging apps such as WhatsApp and China's WeChat. It also includes Facebook Messenger and picture based blogs such as Pinterest and Tumblr.

Both terms in "social media" need to be clearly defined to be able to define such a broad term. "Social" refers to interacting with other people and users by creating, sharing and liking content and information. "Media" refers to an instrument of communication, such as the Internet.

In general, the varying social media channels feature user-generated content (UGC) as their primary foundation and function. Users create specific profiles for the website or the mobile app which are designed to be shared with other users, and eventually brands and companies. On these profiles, users share the specific content, whether it's short 140 character tweets on Twitter or photography on Flickr. Social media facilitate the development of social networks by connecting user profiles with other users. Content can be liked and shared, thereby easily spreading a message from one user to an entire social network.

As a relatively new term, the borders of what constitutes social media are still blurry. For example, some would reason that personal blogs are not part of social media, while others would argue that in fact, they are, as they feature user-generated content. Regardless, social media usage and interaction is booming, and for the 21st-century brand, social media is where you need to be.

CHAPTER 2

COMMON FEATURES OF SOCIAL MEDIA

What connects the different social media platforms? As a rule of thumb, they all contain several varying features that are differently presented from app to app; yet still familiar to most users. The three essential features are listed below.

Profile Page: It's the essential part of a social media platform, as this is the user's way to create content and interact with others. It will usually feature a photo as well as a small description. The depth of these descriptions and profiles varies. Facebook has a relatively extended profile, featuring information about your education and family members and the like, while Instagram only allows you a 140-character description below your name.

News Feed: To see what your friends and your followed companies are posting, you'll have to check the newsfeed. Updated in real-time, your newsfeed features posts from peers and companies, which you can usually 'like', comment on or even share. While different outlets have different names for the posts, such as Twitter referencing a share as a "retweet," the fundamental idea is the same.

Hashtag: While you can easily see your friends content on your feeds, the hashtag allows users to connect their content globally with as little as a symbol "#". For example, if a user has a status update on a great meal at a specific restaurant, the user can create the status update and hashtag it with the brand name, i.e. #DominosPizza or #McDonalds, thereby allowing other users to search the brand name and see the post. Hashtags have been one of the most effective ways to launch campaigns and connects users to a topic of discussion.

CHAPTER 3

WHO USES SOCIAL MEDIA?

It used to be a rule of thumb that only the younger generation was involved in social media. Yet a lot has changed from the early days of Mark Zuckerberg's brainchild Facebook, which was once upon a time restricted to only University students. Adults and children are adding to the profiles of social media users, diversifying the crowd and changing the playing field for marketing.

With 3.4 billion Internet users around the world, 2.3billion of which are active on social media, there doesn't exist just one type of social media users. The profile and platform preference for individual social media users varies across the globe and depends on demographic factors such as age, income, education and area. The average social media user has five accounts and spends around 1 hour and 40 minutes browsing these apps daily, accounting for 28% of their time spent on the Internet.

THE AGE GAME

According to the highly acclaimed Pew Research Center, 74% of all adults online use social media since January 2014. The number is no doubt continuing its growing trend.

That number is even higher for younger adults, with a reported 89% of social media users between the ages of 18-29. While the older generation is catching on slowly but surely, the younger Generation Z, born after the turn of the millennium, is already showing different behaviors for social media usage. The current high schoolers and middle schoolers are turning a cold shoulder to Facebook, the once staple for the youth. Instead, they are increasingly favoring Instagram and Snapchat. That may well be as most of these users remember Facebook as an app, which their parents used, detracting from the once "cool" factor that drove the site to its fame.

THE GENDER GAME

Women may be from Venus and men may hail from Mars, and it shows in their social media usage. While the differences are slight, they are important enough to create the foundations of a specific marketing plan. According to a Nielsen study, women are slightly more involved in social media than men, with 76% of female users compared to 72% male users. Women also spend more time than men on social media, averaging around 10 minutes social networking on their mobile devices compared to a little less than 7 minutes for men.

Women dominate most social media platforms by a slight margin. But they greatly outnumber males on the highly visual digital pin board known as Pinterest. Women also tend to post more on social media, going so far as having more than twice as many posts on their Facebook walls as men. They are also seemingly more popular with an average of 8% more 'friends' than men.

Female Users and Male Users of Social Media Sites pages

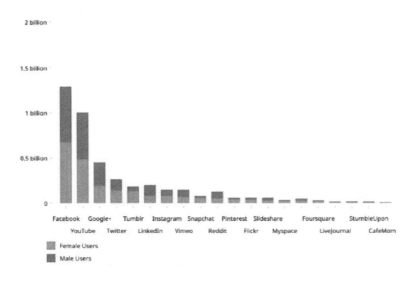

Source: https://14415-presscdn-0-52-pagely.netdna-ssl.com/wp-content/uploads/2015/01/Screen-Shot-2015-01-27-at-3.19.00-PM.png

Men, however, take the lead on the professional networking site LinkedIn, which boasts 24% of the male population compared to 19% of the female population. Men are also more involved on Reddit, and more interactive on music-based social networking sites such as YouTube compared to women.

The most interesting statistic for brands that Nielsen was able to gather was that women are more engaged with brands than men and by a significant landslide. More than half of women use social media to show support or to access deals from brands, which is staggeringly high compared to just 36% of men who do the same. Not only do women rely more on social media to stay up to date with brands; but the ladies are also interacting more with their favored brands by comments and shares.

CHAPTER 4

THE RISE OF THE SMART PHONE

In the early days of Social Media Marketing, the possibilities were restricted to your computer, as the Internet was not yet readily available at your fingertips in your pocket. Without a doubt the biggest push for the increase in SSM was the rise of the Smart Phone. It has also given way to more creative social networking sites, such as for gaming and dating, to name a few. According to Pew Research, nearly two-thirds (64%) of Americans owned a smartphone in 2015. And the younger generation is leading the way towards increased mobile penetration, with 9 out of 10 Millennial owning a smartphone.

Smartphones are the preferred device for users in the U.S., Canada, and the United Kingdom – further proving the need for instant gratification and consumption of information and content. In the

U.S., mobile devices account for 76% of all time spent on social media – a staggering number. And it's no wonder why. Most social media channels have optimized apps that work flawlessly on our phones; limiting the need for interaction on desktops and laptops. In fact, some apps such as Instagram, work significantly better on your phone than on your computer. And some, like Snapchat, work only from your phone. Messaging apps such as WhatsApp and WeChat are also the preferred method of communicating between Millennial. These apps are free to download and offer free messaging when connected to WiFi and without using SMS data.

Smartphones are the future of digital media, with consumption officially breaking the barrier in 2015 in the U.S. with 51% engagement on smartphones compared to 42% on desktops. A key statistic for brands is that consumers spend 89% of their mobile time in apps, and the remaining 11% browsing the web. But that number is highly relevant as Nielsen reported in 2014 that users spend more time browsing the Internet from their phones than from their desktops. The average American adult is surfing the web 27 hours from their desktop computers compared to 34 hours on their smartphones.

Smartphones have dramatically changed the way that people communicate. In your pocket, you hold access to the entire world, whether it be on Twitter, the Internet or another platform. Smartphones allow you to stay connected no matter where you go or what you do.

CHAPTER 5

SOCIAL MEDIA AROUND THE GLOBE

Even though Facebook may be losing its "it" factor with the newcomers to the digital era – it is still the leading social media site around the globe – and that's a serious feat seeing as Facebook is officially banned in China, the world's most populated country.

According to Statista (Appendix A) there are 1,59billion users on Facebook as of April 2016. The second most used social media is the free messaging app WhatsApp, with a total of 1 billion users as of April 2016. That explains why Facebook bought WhatsApp in 2014 for a whopping $22 billion. Not a bad price to own your biggest competitor.

It cannot be dismissed that different parts of the globe interact with social media differently. With government restrictions on some apps, such as in China and Russia, there are different social media platforms in use. For example, Weibo work as a replacement for Facebook and Wechat is being used instead of WhatsApp.

Developing countries have also shown more active users than developed countries. According to research conducted by the Pew Research Center in 2013, Internet users in developing countries are more advanced in their use of social media than the U.S. Social media users in emerging nations demonstrate more interactions and rank higher in overall users for top sites such as Facebook and Twitter.

According to research conducted in 2011 by GlobalWebIndex, social media users in emerging countries were much more highly engaged with their networks – and more likely to actively message with friends and share content while getting involved in groups. Of the eleven countries, which had above global average online users in 2011; nine were developing nations, with the Philippines, Indonesia, and Malaysia rounding out the top three. Social media users also spend more time on the Internet, raking in an impressive average of 5.2 hours daily in the Philippines and Brazil. These numbers can only be expected to rise as the use of smartphones spreads and become more affordable to consumers around the globe.

Global Social Network Penetration

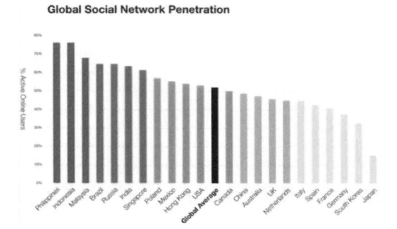

http://wearesocial-net.s3.amazonaws.com/uk/wp-content/uploads/sites/2/2011/06/Global_Penetration.jpg

The role of social media in developing countries cannot be undermined. This was evident in Egypt in 2011 where protestors created an astounding 32,000 Facebook groups for the uprising. It's worth noticing that they did this in a matter of two weeks. Social media, especially Facebook and Twitter, increased communication. It also facilitated the protests that occurred against Egyptian President Hosni Mubarak – so much so that he shut down the Internet for five days, costing an estimated $90 million.

CHAPTER 6

THE DECLINING USE OF TRADITIONAL MEDIA

With the rise of social media in the digital age, a most natural process has occurred in which traditional media, such as television, radio, and newspapers have seen a tremendous decline. As Internet consumption continues to grow rapidly around the globe, these numbers can only be expected to decline. Reasons vary for why consumers decide to switch from traditional media to digital media. But for the most part the underlying principle remains the same – the modernized version of the respective traditional media is more efficient, cheaper and much easier accessed.

Take for example the rise of online streaming services such as Netflix and Amazon Prime. From the comforts of their bed, users can create accounts and share these accounts with family and friends. For a monthly subscription, which is usually far cheaper than cable subscriptions, users have a wide access to shows and movies at their own leisure. They don't feature advertisements, and streaming is the will of the consumer – you can pause and pick up whenever you want, unlike with traditional television. Prime time audiences have dropped nearly 5% while Netflix subscriptions and viewers have only increased.

Similarly, magazines and newspapers, once the staple of print media, have seen a steep decline in use as consumers go paperless and subscribe to online publications of respective news outlets. The fundamental reasons why users are going digital are simple – it's practical, more convenient and cheaper. At the tips of your fingers, you can access your music, your TV shows, and the news – all with as little movement as your thumb.

With the rise of technology, the line between traditional and social media becomes blurred. Most news outlets that had traditional mediums such as The New York Times are now active on social media – posting articles several times per hour on their Facebook newsfeed. The key distinction is that traditional media is a one-way street. There, the consumer are at the receiving end of an outlet, such as the radio or television, where the consumer have a limited way of interacting or responding to the content. Social media on the other hand, offers a two-way street that encourages communication between users, content, news, and brands.

CHAPTER 7

THE WORD, IN REAL TIME

Social media offers something no other traditional media before it has – real time. From live-tweeting presidential debates to sporting events – social media allows users like me and you to lend our opinions, thoughts, jokes and art in real-time. That same theory applies to news outlets. Whereas in the past, a story had to be pitched and created before being carefully released on the radio or in the daily newspapers – social media allows efficient and real-time engagement from news outlets and users alike.

The benefits of this are endless. By updating real time, users are constantly searching their feeds for new content. They are always incentivized to return to the platform to see what they've missed. Brands and consumers can not only directly communicate with one another, but also do it in real time. In fact, most Twitter users expect a response from a brand within one hour of a tweet.

This real-time connection is fostered by hashtags and allows the digital universe and all its inhabitants to connect on the same topics while sitting in the comforts of their own home.

Brands even have a name for real time marketing, calling it 'newsjabbing' whereby their brand is somehow involved in the latest news, and therefore the latest digital conversation. The most famous example would be of Oreo's famous tweet during the 2013 Superbowl. As the most watched televised event annually in America, there was no better time to exploit a mishap than then. With a major power cut disturbing the broadcasting, Oreo's made sure its name was heard with the tweet that was seen around the country.

Oreo Cookie
@Oreo

Power out? No problem.

YOU CAN STILL DUNK IN THE DARK

15,556   6,602

The tweet was retweeted more than 15,000 times and received 18,000 likes on Facebook and more than 5,000 shares. Lisa Mann, the VP of Cookies at Mondelez International noted the importance of real-time marketing when she said :

"Oreo is a real-time brand, a real-time marketer, and we are a part of our culture and the fabric of our community. It is our objective to be as relevant today as we were 100 years ago when we launched."

With 525 million earned impressions, roughly five times the Super Bowl commercial would have, Oreo most definitely managed to stay relevant. Yet real-time marketing has a relatively small window of success. This is because the newsjacking has to happen after the news breaks and immediately before the public excitement grows. If it comes after the excitement and the peak, interest will have already declined, and users won't engage. Timing is therefore crucial for real-time marketing.

CHAPTER 8

WHY COMPANIES NEED SOCIAL

While social networking sites may appear at first glance to be essential for small brands and big corporations – there are endless opportunities for brands. The fact of the matter is clear – customers are online. They might be Tweeting about a brand or asking questions on Facebook. Social media channels provide the optimal layout for brands to engage with customers.

By becoming more active online, your brand can create a sense of trust and bonding with your customers. Not only will your posts appear in the feed together with the customer's friends. It will also enable you to quickly respond to any question that you're customer might have. Opportunities for direct engagement and digital campaigns are endless. Ultimately, a strong online presence will add value to your brand for consumers. Much like a real relationship, brands can foster direct and personal engagements with users, thereby perpetuating their brand and further establishing themselves.

There are clear benefits to engaging with consumers, and ultimately it will create advocacy for your brand. As peer reviews are becoming the go-to for rating products, it is essential for brands to create a positive and active online presence. You can't get ahead of the competitors or the game if you aren't playing it. Without a doubt, social media marketing is the best way for a brand to reach its consumers through the feedback, interactions, and relationships it fosters.

How to Measure Success & Social Media Metrics

Measuring the success of social media campaigns and posts can be quite difficult. On the superficial layer, statistics of shares and likes are easy to obtain. But they don't dig deeper into the true impact of a campaign or a post that went viral. Several different factors are of key importance, and it truly depends on your situation which statistics matter.

Reach will measure the size of an audience that you're communicating with, while *impressions* look at how many people saw your posts. *Engagement* is the total number of likes, shares, and comments on a particular post. *Visits* count each time a person visits your distinct page while *unique visits* count each person only once.

Not all metrics are created the same, and it is important to figure out which you need for your specific business.

It is relatively easy to keep track of a **click-through rate**, i.e. the indicator that your message was important enough to spark interest for your online audience. It is important however to calculate the **bounce rate** to better understand your Return on Investment (ROI.) The bounce rate refers to the percentage of page visitors who leave your site after only viewing one page. Ideally, a person would browse through your page indefinitely. But with shrinking attention spans, this is hardly the case. Google Analytics will provide this service to you.

In addition to the importance of social media mentions, it is vital to track your **share of voice**. While **mentions** indicate how many people are talking to and about your business on social media – the share of voice tells you what percentage of mentions within the industry are about your brand. And equally importantly, what percentage of those are about your competition. Hoot Suite Analytics can track your mentions as well as those of your competitors. After you add them up, simply divide the sum by the total of industry mentions, and multiply by 100 to get a percentage. Hooray for simple math!

Conversion rate is the way to measure action, i.e. the number of people who achieved a desired result, either by purchasing a product, signing up for a trial or any other goal that was set for the campaign. But conversions are not always the key metric as a well-shared Facebook post will not necessarily encourage consumer to purchase a product – but instead create a deeper bond between the brand and the consumer. Your conversion rate is the ratio of comments per post to the number of overall followers of page likes. This will ultimately determine how much of your audience is engaged enough to add their voice to your social media content. As the founder of the metric Avinash Kaushik, a digital marketer at

Google, said: "Is what you are saying interesting enough to spark the most social of all things: a conversation?"

Similarly, the **amplification rate** measures the number of shares on social media against the number of overall followers of page likes. It provides a deeper examination of how strong of an impact your post had, not just in shares; but shares relative to your followers. To get this number, simply use the number of times your content was shared and divide it by the total number of followers, and multiply by 100.

The **applause rate** is to likes what the amplification rate is to shares. While likes are a very valuable social media currency, they don't offer too much insight as a stand-alone metric. The applause rate, therefore, gives you the ratio of likes per post to the number of overall followers, or page likes. It's a simple statistic to calculate: simply divide the number of likes by the number of page followers and multiply by 100.

The afro-mentioned statists are relatively easy to calculate on your own. But in the age of digital, it's vital to use online analytics services. There are countless different sites, for free and paid, that offer different services depending on your needs. Keep in mind that most social media platforms do offer their own analytics, usually located on the dashboard. All the major players including Facebook, Pinterest, Twitter and the like offer insights on the specific performance of specific posts and overall progress.

However, an ample amount of websites and tools exist to help you manage and track the success of your brand regarding social media usage. **Google Analytics**, for example, is one of the most popular tools for analyzing website traffic. *Klout* gives your company a score from 0 to 100 regarding your influence on major social media channels. *Hootsuit* is the most widely used platform for managing social media. It lets you keep track of what people are saying. *Google Insights* and *Google Trends* are effective at measuring and comparing changes to search volume for your brand against competitor's brands. This can lend you an insight on the ability to engage customers on social media relative to your competition. *Marketo* or *Coverto* on the other hand will measure how many social interaction or web page visits it takes before a prospect becomes a customer. And while mentions are good, some can be negative. Not all publicity is good publicity and tools such as *SocialMention* or *Meltwater* help you measure the sentiment of the conversation around your brand, which in turn helps you maintain a positive brand image. These are just some of the online platforms to help you manage your social media presence and keep track of vital stats.

CHAPTER 9

SEARCH ENGINE OPTIMIZATION & SOCIAL MEDIA MARKETING

Social media marketing and search engines, such as Google, are inextricably linked through Search Engine Optimization (SEO).

SEO is the process of maximizing the number of visitors to a particular website through ensuring that the website appears higher on the list of results returned by the search engine. As a rule of thumb, the earlier a website or brand appears on the list of the search results on a page – the more visitors it will receive from search engine users. This could in effect greatly increase your social media reach.

In effect, improving your social media reach and engagement would organically boost your ranking on search engines, thereby bringing more people to your social media site. Social sharing is key to increasing your ranking for search engines.

Strong content on social media with bold, catchy titles that feature keywords will feed into the engine and amplify the reach of your brand. Google focuses on two main factors when ranking for search queries – relevance and authority. Relevance refers to how appropriately it meets the needs of a given search query while the authority is how trustworthy the source is. On a simple level; the higher authority links you create and own – the higher you will rank on a search engine. Social media plays a vital role in this because of its flawless ability to distribute content at forest fire rates, which could land in the hands (or better said, the profiles) of journalists, editors and bloggers who would then reference your link. It has the feel of a middle school popularity contest, but Search Engine Optimization is vital to increasing the digital presence of your brand.

The bottom line for the intersection of SEO and SSM is shareability. Creating and publishing content that has a high potential for becoming viral and being shared is the key to improving your ranking on search engines. Titles, keywords and phrases that are trending and easily searchable will be of most benefit to increasing visibility of your brand. Titles are limited to 75 characters while descriptions are limited to 160 – so pay special attention to those. Keyword optimization is vital for a link to make its way to the top of the search engine. Timing is vital, whether it's seasonal or related to a specific event – too early and the people won't catch it or too late, and the people will already be on to the next.

Pro Tips

Joseph Haslam, senior director of social SEO at Education Dynamics, has narrowed down four key characteristics for social media to be optimized for SEO. Content should be segmented, searchable, snackable and shareable.

It should be segmented in that way that your content must address the needs of your segmented audience, one that you know well. Hootsuit and Twitter will allow you to monitor what is currently trending, thereby giving you insight on how to focus your article. Your content should be searchable, which means that keywords need to be referenced and used. Content needs to be snackable, which is not to say it has to be sweet and crunch but rather:

- Well-organized

- Sectioned with labeled content

- And supported with ample amount of visual aid such as charts, illustrations, gifs and video.

It will be this type of content that readers will come back to munch on. And finally, your content needs to be shareable. Tags and hashtags are an effective starting point to cover your bases. But more than that you will need to use your metrics to keep track of your shares and interactions on social media in order to learn what's working for your users and what needs to be improved.

PART 2

SOCIAL MEDIA

PLATFORMS

CHAPTER 10

GENERAL TIPS FOR SOCIAL MEDIA

Social media platforms may seem as if they all serve the same purpose – and as a baseline, they DO connect users and profiles to each other and brands. But each unique platform offers different services and tools that better connect users to each other. Some work heavily on images, such Pinterest and Instagram while others such as Snapchat rely on video content. Different social media platforms offer different benefits for your brand. But that doesn't necessarily mean your brand has to be featured on all platforms to be relevant. Quality is more important than quantity, so choose your platforms wisely.

The leading social media platforms will be discussed. Key demographics assessed for each social media platform will be addressed as well as marketing advice – as a one-size-fits-all plan won't work for different platforms.

✓ Remember the Holidays and Big Events

In order to be the topic of conversation, you need to stay relevant. That means keeping up with (and staying ahead) of the latest trends and big events. Remember the holidays and be sure to post relevant content for the holiday seasons or big international events such as the Olympics or Fashion Week. Coca-Cola made good use of this idea during the Sochi Olympics with their campaign #CokeGames, which asked followers to play games and upload videos of games such as Bottle Cap Hockey, Coke Curling and the favorite Ice Cube Ski Jump. The incentive was a simple $100 gift card. Choose events that are relevant to your brand. But don't forget the big national holidays and international events.

✓ Crowdsource Your Next Idea

Don't forget that your customers are often times the ones that can lead you to your most profound company changes. Be sure to listen to their responses and see what you can change in order to improve their customer experience.

✓ Keep it lighthearted

Comedy goes a long way, and if it fits your brand, have some fun with it. If you are a product-based company, ask users to post pictures of themselves. Don't take yourself so seriously that you can't have fun. Skittles, for example, is a brand that does humor well. Their status can vary from random to absurd, such as "Really boring pirates carry pigeons on their shoulders." Either way, it's sure to get your followers commenting and engaging with your content.

✓ Follow the 70/20/10 Rule

As a rule of thumb, the 70/20/10 rule is good to keep in mind. The majority of your content should be brand and business building – as in content that's meaningful information for your followers. Content shared from other sources should make up around 20% while the remaining 10% can be self-promotional. By incorporating shared content, you can cultivate a deeper and more meaningful image of your brand that extends beyond just the basic product or service you offer. Show off your interests and make sure to share content from other sites, which will in turn increase views.

✓ Customer Service Rules All

Customer service is essential on social media platforms. Users expect their questions to be answered quickly and directly. Feedback is key to fostering trust and a sense of brand loyalty. This way you will boost engagement and show your customers that the brand cares about them.

CHAPTER 11

DO'S AND DON'TS TO INTERACTING WITH YOUR FOLLOWERS ON SOCIAL MEDIA

DO

✓ **Do respond to all questions, negative or positive.**

This includes comments, direct messages, and other commentary. Always give it your best shot at turning the negative comments into possible positives. And if the situation can't be rectified, offer your condolences and make up for the hurt feelings with discounts or coupons for future purchases. Users expect to have responses relatively quickly after they post comments or questions, so make sure you are always updating your sites.

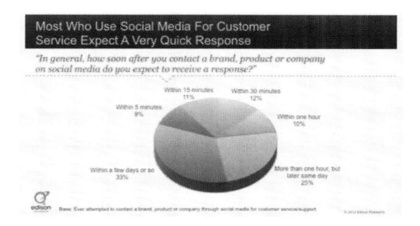

✓ Do maintain one voice across all of your platforms.

It can be expected that your followers are keeping up with your brand on several different channels. Make sure that your message is consistent and clear on the different channels and streamlined with your voice.

✓ Do have a personality.

The problem with social media lies in the clutter. It can be difficult to have your voice heard off all of the noise created by users and brands on social media. Therefore, make sure to stand out from the rest. Create a voice that is unique to you. A little bit of humor or going that extra step in following-up with customers on social media can be game changing in establishing your presence.

✓ Do share the key information over all your platforms.

If you have an event created on Facebook, be sure to share that information on all your platforms. You can easily share a link from your Facebook event to your Twitter page or create a separate Instagram post for the event. Use your different platforms to highlight different parts of your event or of the message you want to relay to your followers.

✓ Do experiment.

You can never fully know what will resonate with an audience. Whether it's a cute video of a kitten or a puppy or a serious post, different content strikes audiences at different times. Accept the challenge and see what works best for you and continue to evolve your social media strategy.

✓ Do publish content that is mobile friendly.

As users continue to bring their social media with them from their desktops to their phones, keep in mind that your content will be viewed from different devices. Make sure that your content is mobile friendly, and that your website functions well on smartphones.

✓ Do remember the 'social' in social media.

At the end of the day, social media is about social relationships. Platforms give people and brands a possibility to create and foster relationships. Engage with your followers and don't forget about them after they follow you. High-quality followers who engage more (by sharing and commenting) are far more valuable to your brand than a high but empty number of likes.

✓ Do match the right content to the right platform.

Not all social media networks were created equally, and each different platform can offer you something another platform can't. Keep in mind that Facebook is a causal network while LinedIn is a professional network. The content that is shared on those would not always be the same. LinkedIn is no place for a funny cat video, but Facebook is.

DON'T

- **Don't over flood the news feeds of your followers.**

There's a Goldilocks type method of keeping your followers entertained and not crowding their feeds with your content.

- **Don't like your own posts.**

It simply is a rule of social media – you don't like your own posts. Of course you actually like them, I mean, you posted them. But don't break the unspoken rule of liking your own content.

- **Don't spam.**

Social media was not intended for spamming, and your profile shouldn't resemble a spam folder. Keep the content invigorating and original, and avoid having too much promotional content on your profiles. Otherwise, you run the risk of looking like a spam account, which will surely yield to a decrease in followers.

- **Don't write in all caps.**

Once upon a time caps, i.e. writing with all upper case letters, was a means to an end in showing your passion for a topic. Nowadays, writing with the caps lock on is an indicator that you are very upset about something. Make sure that your message is not lost in the tone and subtext of your writing, and stay away from the caps.

- **Don't delete negative comments.**

Deleting negative comments spells a PR disaster down the line. Addressing negative feedback head-on shows that your company cares about its customers and is willing to tackle issues. As social media is about fostering relationships, it's highly counterintuitive to just delete negative feedback. After all, if someone walked into your store with a complaint, you wouldn't just turn your back on them. You would address the issue at hand. The same mentality should unfold on social media.

- **Don't spread yourself thin.**

To have a strong social media presence, you don't need to be on all platforms. While Facebook is a good start for most businesses, your brand may not need to have a presence on Tumblr or a big following on Twitter. It is important to choose your social media platforms wisely and pursue them well, rather than trying all platforms and not being able to maintain them at the top levels.

- **Don't let just anyone represent your brand.**

Having a brand ambassador or a collaboration with a brand influencer can be powerful in promoting your brand. But brand influencers and ambassadors have to be carefully selected. They will be the connection between your brand and your audience, and will inevitably come to mind when people think of your brand. Make sure to pick someone who embodies your brand to the best of their abilities — and someone you can trust.

- **Don't automate your message across your platforms.**

While it may seem like an easy time saver, having the same wording for an Instagram post, a Twitter tweet, and a Google Plus update is highly unstateful and lazy. If you don't care enough to write out a sentence or two about your brand, why should followers care enough to read it? Vary your tone and your message in order to keep your audience on their toes.

CHAPTER 12

THE RISE OF SOCIAL INFLUENCERS

Social media has brought with a new way of marketing, involving a very personable sales person. Instagram Influencers are bloggers, models, creative and all around spokespersons who have risen to fame on the social media platform. With followers ranging from anywhere in the low thousands to the several million, there is no way to talk about Instagram without talking about Instagram Influencers. Often female and usually beautiful, these starlets have made their claim to fame from their phones. They're stylish and fashionable or fit and healthy, but they're always promoting something. Take for example fashion blogger Chiara Ferragni, the Italian fashion blogger who has more than 6 million followers on Instagram. With her rise to fame in fashion, the young law student has now amassed fans across the globe, which has landed her with jaw-dropping deals from designer labels eager to use her Instagram account (and the followers that it reaches) with their products.

Chiara Feragni, as featured in InStyle Magazine
http://www.instyle.com/news/blonde-salad-blogger-chiara-ferragni-interview-style-secrets-instagram

Social Media Influencers aren't celebrities, but they eventually do attain celebrity status. While celebs such as Selena Gomez with her more than 102 million followers on Instagram can serve as influencers for brands, she isn't a classic Instagram influencer. Both celebrities and Instagram influencers can promote brands and sponsor ads, but Instagram Influencers grew out of their own accord. They are the gateway between brands and users and are often paired off with fashion labels, make-up brands, and wellness brands. Influencers have even made a living off of their careers as promoters, such as the two Dutch girls who run the Instagram account "WeLikeBali", in which they travel the island of the Gods one luxurious villa at a time, promoting each home with carefully curated images of paradise.

The rise of Instagram Influencers may seem absurd to some, but the logic behind it is simple – people don't generally want to see ads on their feeds. Social media platforms are intimate online spaces for users and getting bombarded with ads takes away from that experience. The fact of the matter is that people don't want to see adds on their feeds and are searching for organic content. This is where influencers come in. They are able to generate visually satisfying and seemingly organic content that simultaneously promotes a brand. Organic content and advertising meet where social media Influencers start.

And micro-influencers shouldn't be overlooked by brands either. Some of the more followed Influencers are simply not affordable. A single 4x4 sponsored image on Selena Gomez's feed will run you about $500,000. That's not feasible unless you're Coca-Cola or Nike. Smaller bloggers are still able to promote content and products — just on a more centralized market.

Social Influencers can be broken down into six specific categories. These categories are definitive and are sure to grow as the digital world develops. But for now, there are six defining categories for Social Influencers.

1. The Well-Rounded *LIFE*

It's not just about a healthy diet or fitness regime. These are people living the wholesome, healthy life, from daybreak until they hit the hay.

Brands that use this archetype include Adidas, Banana Republic, and Smartwater.

Ex: Hannah Bronfman's Instagram account has a 360-degree look into her healthy life.

2. *THE TEAM PLAYER*

Online comedy has skyrocketed with YouTube as a leading platform for individuals and groups to let their funny bones shine, and brands are taking notice.

Brands using this archetype include Coca-Cola and Dunkin Donuts.

Ex: Jake Paul's Team 10 works with several influencers that share content with 18 million daily views across channels.

3. *The Personal Touch*

Fashion icons with their taste and personalities that attract millions of followers.

Brands using this archetype: GQ, Target, ColourPop

Ex: Jenn Im's has an audience of more than 1 million Instagram followers and 1.7 million subscribers to her YouTube channel.

https://www.youtube.com/watch?v=ntzQ-EwxU4k

4. The Gaming Star

Brands are taking notice of the big personas behind the joysticks. E-sport players are all the rage amongst new brands.

Brands using this archetype: Slim Jim, Tinder, Red Bull

Ex: Matt Haag (aka Nadeshot) has 2.7 million YouTube subscribers and 1.9 million Twitter followers.

http://mytopgadgets.com/20-richest-e-sports-players/17/

5. *THE QUIRKY COOK*

While cooking used to be reserved for well scripted Afternoon television, online chefs have taken advantage of humanizing the kitchen.

Brands using this archetype: Barilla, Subaru, Dish, Hormel

Ex: Rosanna Pension's baked sweets for geeks have amassed her 7.2 million loyal fans on YouTube and 2.1 million followers on Instagram.

https://www.pinterest.com/maximumride21/youtube-cooking/

6. THE ADVENTURER

As Millennial give up on material goods and spend their money on traveling, influencers are keeping tabs of their adventurous lives that tell stories across varying platforms.

Brands using this archetype: Marriott, Skype

Ex: 35% of Jackson Harries' 1.8 million Instagram followers have stayed engaged for more than three years.

https://www.tumblr.com/search/harries%20jack

CHAPTER 13

THE IMPORTANCE OF ORGANIC CONTENT

Organic content will be vital to the success of your brand on social media. As generations have grown up with sponsored ads on traditional media such as television and radio, social media brought a new era of advertising, which is native and organic. Banner ads are becoming less and less efficient in increasing brand awareness. More often than not, sponsored ads are simply "ex-ed" out of, scrolled over or deleted. With apps such as AdBlocker on many Internet browsers, it goes to show what people don't want – sponsored content. Most organic social media posts aren't directly selling their followers something. Because selling is rarely interesting enough to drive significant engagements.

That's when social media can be the perfect brand ambassador for your brand. Creating a brand persona behind the brand name is key in building your following and reaching a new audience. Organic and native content show users that you are indeed creative and resourceful, and want to engage with customers on more than just a purchase decision. Organic posts are the foundation for community management, and your voice can be heard by thousands of people when you start the right discussions on the right platforms.

In effect, social media is about telling a story. The story of who your brand is and what it stands for. This story won't be told all on one platform, but will utilize a specific combination of several different platforms to best showcase your narrative to the world. With so many brands using social media as a platform to pitch their products rather than engage their followers, it pays to be the one building real connections with your audience.

CHAPTER 14

OPTIONS FOR PAID TRAFFIC

While organic content should be your main aim on social media, paid traffic can help increase the viewership of the content and overall help your brand awareness. Keep in mind that this paid traffic does not include buying followers or likes. That is an empty method used by some social influencers and brands to increase their numbers. However, their engagement will always remain low. It leads to a poor audience and is an overall bad strategic decision. And in the end, higher engagement is more valuable than higher likes.

Paid social media in the context that we will discuss is the implementation of paid ads and marketing for the purpose of delivering content to relevant audience members. These members are actually interested in what your selling and not a fake account used to increase your stats. When you are using paid social media, you are leveraging social media ads to drive traffic by putting money behind your social media posts. Furthermore, paying for ads allow you to target a specific audience and increase your overall social media reach, i.e. the estimated number of people exposed to your content.

There are several different strategic points in your brand's life when you should considering paid traffic options.

1 . When you are building your audience from the ground up

Of course, building your audience from the ground up can work organically, but that is living life in the slow lane. Using paid options will speed up the process of reaching people who follow your content and who share it. Organically, you can share and post your content on different platforms and engage with potential followers. However, you are limited to the natural process of things, which could be quite slow. Consider investing in paid traffic early on to create awareness from the get-go.

2 . When you are diversifying the demographic of your audience

Once you have reached your target demographic, it is likely that you might consider expanding into different groups. Paid traffic could be the solution to your problems if you are considering expanding your brand into different locations, where your current followers are not based. Geotargeting is especially useful as it allows you to create ads in specific locations as narrow as zip codes, which further increase your specific target audience.

3. When you are looking to scale your social platforms with a similar audience

Once you have a sizeable social media following, it is natural to get stuck due to the law of diminishing returns. At the beginning of your social media life, you may see huge amounts of followers daily. But further down the line, these numbers might begin to trickle and eventually plateau. Once you hit a certain number – and for many companies that number is around 10,000 followers – there is a noticeable lag in increase and growth. In order to continue stimulating growth, paid advertisements are a sure fire way to get people to continue liking you site.

4. When you want to increase your organic reach

The irony is not lost on us – in order to increase your organic traffic, you need to invest in paid traffic. But there is a method to the madness. There is much competition for brands to get their share of voice in on the clutter that can often be associated with social media. The sheer volume of content posted by the minute is in direct opposition to your content. So while users may be liking your content, it doesn't necessarily mean that your content is showing up in their feeds. If you want to grow the audience that gets to see your organic content, you will need to invest in paid traffic. It will increase the frequency of which consumers are seeing your content. In turn, this lead to more information being shared about promotions or offers.

It should be noted that there is a difference in high traffic and high-quality traffic. If you are new to the social media game, all the matters for the moment is high traffic. You want as many people as possible to see your online presence and your content. However, if you have already been established in the digital sphere, your focus should be on generating high-quality traffic. The quality of the audience you build is important, and you don't just want random likes. Ideally, likers would engage with your brand and eventually purchase your service or product. Keep in mind that paid ads on social media can only be as good as the organic content. The ads can bring the users to your site or profile, but what will make the users stay is not the ads but rather the content itself.

Paid social media traffic can be an outstanding tool in building your digital presence. Timing is of utmost importance, and you cannot just purchase ads at any point in time of your business. Paid search traffic is a good alternative when you can't quite generate enough organic traffic. Consider your business goals, and whether they are to generate new leads or increasing awareness – and from there, whether you have reached a time when utilizing paid social media traffic would be the right option for you.

CHAPTER 15

CAUSE-RELATED MARKETING

A recent trend that has permeated both traditional media and social media is the rise of cause-related marketing. Brands are aligning themselves with social causes and non-profits in order to support a message that goes above and beyond their brand. While brands don't necessarily need to sponsor a philanthropic cause, their message could simply be an empowering one that goes deeper than the surface. Positive and uplifting messages are very common for the beauty and fashion industries. For example, such as Dove's winning Real Beauty campaign, in which the viewer often forgets that they are watching an advertisement as the message of the ad is not strictly based on the product – but rather on a concept. Your brand should go more than just selling a product; it should empower and promote a cause. GAP's never-ending campaign with (RED) showcases the power of a brand when it ties itself to a cause.

https://allheartscamodad.wordpress.com/2012/06/19/product-red-gap-leather-bracelet/

CHAPTER 16

UNIQUE SOCIAL MEDIA PLATFORMS

FACEBOOK

The original social media platform, Facebook, is still the frontrunner is social media usage – across all key demographics regardless of age, location or gender. Facebook is the ideal blend of visual and verbal context, as it allows brands to post photos, videos and an unrestricted amount of text. Users can comment, like and share the posts and even direct message a brand. Brands are even going so far as to replace their unique websites with Facebook sites. This is because their Facebook profile offers everything that a site would – including contact information, reviews and opening hours.

There are different ways to market on Facebook, including your brand page, ads, and groups.

Pages are the most crucial for a brand and essential in the modern marketing game. They function similar to personal profiles. But users can like the page, which means they will automatically receive updates in their Newsfeeds about the page. Recently, Facebook added a feature where users can follow a brand but not "Like" it; meaning they don't outrightly show their support but the content still shows up in their feeds. Unlike personal profiles, there are no limits to how many people like your page. For example, Nike has more than 27 million Likes.

Facebook pages are easy to set up and manage and are free of costs. There are some rules of thumb on how to use the page.

Profile Picture – Your profile picture should be your brand logo, simple as that.

Cover Photo – Should be a picture of your current campaign. There are no restrictions, but the photo should be of high quality and capture you're a visitors attention.

About Section – Right beneath your company logo is featured an "About" section. The key is to keep it short and sweet. Facebook doesn't need to be formal so keep it light and relevant to readers. You can use the same text from your website or blog if it's fitting, but be sure to fill in all the other information as well, so your site is comprehensive and doesn't leave users with more questions.

Once the initial setup of your Facebook Page is done, the real fun can start. Posting content on your timeline is crucial as it will keep audiences aware. But the key is not to clutter the feed of your followers as they will be less likely to engage with the content. The content you post on your timeline doesn't always have to be 100%

relevant to your upcoming events or promotions – but can also feature links on causes your support or profiles of people in your local community that you support. Allow your Facebook profile to be more than just a brand. Breathe character and life into it so that people will be able to relate and connect with the brand on a more meaningful level.

While it's relatively easy to create a Facebook profile, the real deal happens when you need to start promoting and expanding your reach. Below are several tips for increasing the effectiveness of your Facebook account.

Optimize your Facebook page for SEO and like

It's most likely that your Facebook page will be the starting point for users interacting with your brand. Therefore, it should rank highly in both Google and Facebook searches, so your current and prospective customers can find you with ease.

- ✓ Be sure to use descriptive words in your About section, especially keywords that customers will type into search queries.

- ✓ Be sure to include your website URL in your description.

- ✓ Ensure that you are in the appropriate category or business, i.e. distinguishing between a walk in business and an online business.

Use Facebook groups to engage with your target market

Facebook pages are vital in your social media marketing strategy – but using them efficiently is key. Facebook offer users the opportunity to make "Groups," wherein users with common interests can share knowledge, links tips and questions. Groups are

Facebook's answer to Forums. When used correctly, groups can tremendously increase traffic to your Facebook page.

- ✓ Create your own Facebook group. You can network with loyal fans and invite new customers to join in on the discussion. Creating your own group will allow you to interact with your customer segment in a more personable and effective way.

- ✓ Join existing Facebook groups and stay active! Make sure your voice is heard and respond to relevant posts and questions.

Encourage social sharing through Facebook buttons and plugins

Ideally, Facebook will create more traffic to your website. But that means that all of your content on your site should be shareable on Facebook, with the plugin readily available.

- ✓ Ensure that all content on your site has a Like and Share button.

Post Strategically

Let's clear the air – there is no perfect time to post or perfect day for optimal reach and engagement. While there has been an ample amount of research done on the best posting times, it will be up to you to determine which works best for your page.

- ✓ There is no such thing as the perfect day to post. Research has suggested that Thursdays and Fridays may result in higher engagement. But use this information as a starting point for your posting practices and see from there.

✓ Cinderella ran out of time but you surely won't. The time of your posts truly depends on your business as different categories would have different times. For example, cooking and food related content may be more readily shared around dinner and consumption times. Furthermore, timing is tricky as your brand expands across time zones, so don't get too hung up on the perfect time. Of course, your content will be less viewed and shared when it's posted at witching hour, so be active during the hours that your customers are active. Some research has suggested that posting between 1 pm and 3 pm is optimal for sharing, so use that as a starting point.

✓ How often you post, is more important than what time and what day of the week you post. Finding the perfect balance is tricky. If you post too little, your audiences will not stay engaged and won't be able to maintain a social connection. On the other hand, posting too often will clutter the feeds of your audience and will disengage them. Two posts per day were found to be the ideal number, so around 14 posts per week. Again, this is a rule of thumb and depends on your company and the message you want to share with your audience.

Consider paid options to optimize your reach

While it's entirely feasible to maintain your Facebook organically without any additional charges, the social media platform does offer paid alternatives to boost your performance.

✓ Boost Posts – Boosting a post will increase the visibility of the posts in user's newsfeeds. With so much content being created and shared on Facebook, a post is easily lost in the sphere of the Internet. Using boosts, you can choose to have your post shown to your page fans, friends of your fans or other people based on targeting. Targeting options include interests (which users choose themselves), age, gender and location.

✓ Promoted posts: Promoted posts are accessed from your Facebook Ads Manager. Promoting a post requires more thought and should usually serve a specific goal, such as; increasing traffic to your website or selling a product. Compared to boosting a post, promoting a post gives your more choice on specific targeting goals. A helpful tool for deciding when to promote a post is the "STIR" method. Before promoting a post, ask yourself these four questions:

S – Shelf Life: Will the post be relevant 4-days from publication?

T- Time: Has it been at least six hours since publication?

I – Impact: Does the post include a link or another call-to-action that creates a desirable customer behavior, beyond a simple "like"?

R – Result: Has the post exceeded a 1% engagement rate (likes + comments + shares / total fans)

Learning from the best
With so many millions of users and profiles, it's hard to know where to look for inspiration from brands on Facebook. Mavrck.co narrowed down the top brand pages on Facebook from the first 30 days in 2016, based on engagements. Now we have dissected what makes these brands stand out from the rest. Sure, you might not have their big marketing budgets, but you can take their cues on what to do and how to do it.

- Starbucks: Starbucks stays on top. And the reasons for that don't directly stem from big ad spending. Starbucks responds to every single fan comment, whether it's a drink clarification or a personal experience. The constant engagement with fans within the comment threads further fosters a brand relationship between fans and often leads to discussion threads that look like fan forums.

  o Take- Away: Stay active and interact with your fans.

- Coca-Cola: Within 30 days, the international soda company posted 19 video posts, with a combined 55,000 shares. Coca-Cola was quick to pick up on Facebook's new algorithm change, which strongly favors video content. The priority for Coca-Cola is clear: create engaging and high-quality video content.

  o Take-Away: Bring in the video.

- MTV: Sure, it' an entertainment brand and the content options are relatively endless, which is why MTV beats most brands by the sheer volume of posts. But only 2 out of every 10 posts directly promotes the brand itself. This allows users to feel connected with the brand as it posts much like a friend on their Newsfeeds. A friend that has perfected the art of sneak-peek content that encourages click-through.

  o Take-Away: Get personal and post engaging content that goes beyond just your brand.

- Samsung: With a heavy tech audience, Samsung knows just what to do to get the blood racing of their fans. That includes hashtags that make campaigns, as #TheNextGalaxy did back in January 2016, and launched 7 videos over the course of the month to generate feedback. The videos often tell the story directly of their consumers that make their content go viral.

o   Take-Away: Get personal. Know your audience, and bring them into your campaigns.

- NBA: While football and baseball may be the nation's pastime, basketball is leading the Facebook world. The NBA has over 31 million likes and their secret to their growing audience is *snackability*. All of the content shared on their page is posted directly to Facebook, instead of linked posts that direct to another site. The NFL and the MLB take the latter approach and obviously don't fare as well on Facebook. The NBA posts game footage highlights and fan photos, a double win as it ensures fan engagement.

o   Take-Away: Make your content snackable and easily to use.

TOP BRANDS ON FACEBOOK

RANK BRAND	TOTAL FACEBOOK FANS	TOTAL POSTS (LAST 30 DAYS)	TOTAL MICRO-INFLUENCER COMMENTS	TOTAL ENGAGEMENTS DRIVEN	AVERAGE INFLUENCER INDEX
1 Starbucks	36,008,149	50	249	20,334	85.77
2 Coca-Cola	96,231,318	50	136	6,917	57.79
3 MTV	48,502,138	172	566	22,254	56.65
4 Samsung Mobile	25,532,458	35	125	4,948	44.6
5 NBA	28,108,683	524	1,359	18,835	35.39
6 KFC	39,928,551	15	166	4,224	34.62
7 WWE	29,489,945	942	3,492	34,211	32.91
8 Nike	23,627,379	50	162	3,334	31.55
9 Target	23,179,057	50	223	4,346	30.75
10 United Airlines	859,768	50	284	3,960	29.46
11 Red Bull	44,833,222	1,150	244	4,810	27.72
12 Walmart	32,702,630	50	516	3,341	26.04
13 Visa	19,753,812	50	106	2,948	25.86
14 Playstation	37,646,130	68	187	2,917	23.49
15 Dove	25,307,381	50	181	2,316	20.28
16 Southwest Airlines	4,894,152	26	141	2,671	19.98
17 Oreo	41,747,899	50	213	2,019	17.83
18 Heineken	20,310,549	47	153	1,967	17.75
19 McDonald's	61,927,777	18	223	3,002	17.51
20 Dodge	3,362,781	71	873	7,293	15.47
21 Intel	25,205,280	52	140	1,636	13.43
22 Disney	50,597,050	119	378	1,506	11.49
23 BMW	19,108,599	58	640	3,548	11.05
24 Bud Light	7,438,522	50	161	1,197	10.1
25 MasterCard	13,518,807	50	97	895	8.49

MAVRCK ▶

Facebook Summary

Facebook is your gateway into social media. It's the most basic and fundamental of all the platforms. Easy to use, it's the platform from which you can jumpstart your foray into other social media platforms, such as Instagram or LinkedIn, which often connect your profile to their profiles. Facebook is an essential social media you have to use for any business.

INSTAGRAM

Recently acquired by Facebook, Instagram is the visual alternative to Facebook. Instagram works similarly to Facebook, but it's much less wordy. As in just barely. Users upload edited photographs to their profiles and can scroll through their feeds to see the latest updates of their friend's photographs. Instagram has been optimized for the phone and is thus a mobile app. The website is not often used by desktops, which is starkly different from Facebook which is both easy to use on a desktop or on your mobile app. Instagram has been heralded as the creative outlet. While Facebook lets users posts status updates about their dinner and work dramas, Instagram is usually drama free. It has been hailed as the creative cousin of the varying social media platforms. With 60% of users logging in daily, Instagram is the second most engaged network after Facebook.

Demographics

As it is heavily visually based, the initial audience of Instagram appealed more for women. Over the recent years, that gap has closed somewhat. But women are still heavier users of Instagram than men by **DATA**. As a relatively newer app than its counterpart Facebook, Instagram caters better to the Millennial and Generation Z demographics – so much so that in fact 90% of Instagram users are under the age of 35. Instagram is vital for the younger generation, and 32% of teenagers would list it as their most important social media.

As of March 2016, 48.8% of brands were active on Instagram. That number is expected to rise to 70.7% by 2017. That's a key statistic and motivator for up and coming brands. Especially since 90% of the top 100 brands in the world have Instagram accounts and 50% of Instagramers follow brands, making them the social networkers who are most likely to do so. And that may be for a good reason as engagement with brands on Instagram is 10 times higher than Facebook – 54 times higher than its visual counterpart Pinterest and 84 times higher than Twitter. The incentive for product-based brands to use Instagram is even higher. This is because over one-third of Instagram users have used their mobile to purchase a produce online, making them 70% more likely to do so than non-users.

People are more attracted to visuals than words. Instagram offers another level of intimacy for brands with consumers as they are sharing photos and moments rather than just comments and questions.

Advertising on Instagram

Sponsored ads appearing in feeds are a recent addition to Instagram. While Facebook features sponsored ads peppered throughout users feeds, Instagram features the more seamless alternative known as native ads, which means they blend right into the feed. Sponsored ads are the same format and size as users posts, and therefore are less disruptive and more likely to be viewed by users than other forms of ads. With a range of call-to-action buttons, such as "Learn more," Download," or "Shop Now," the ads can be very useful in maximizing conversions.

Unfortunately, as of now the ads are not readily available to all brands. There isn't much official information on the pricing of an Instagram ad. However, some sources have said that they can cost up to $1 million USD per mont – a number reserved for the top dogs in the game. As of now, sponsored Instagram ads won't be the way for small business to create a strong Instagram presence. But thankfully there are other ways to promote your brand on the social media platform.

Methods to Promote your Brand on Instagram

1) **Host a Giveaway.** Giveaways a sure-fire way to get people to interact with your brand on Instagram. Paired with a clever hashtag and an unbeatable prize, it's a classic way method with a social media twist.

2) **Collaborate with an Instagram Influencer.** Instagram Influencers are the new marketing tools for word of mouth. Their high numbers of loyal followers appreciate their organic content and take their recommendations on products, travel tips, beauty advice and anything else to heart. It'll be a sure-fire way to get your product out to your target market.

3) **Hashtag, hashtag, hashtag.** While Hashtags are important to use on all platforms, Instagram's search tool is optimized for hashtags. It's important to hashtag relevant topics for your post and to keep it broad and simple. If you are selling a beauty product, keep the tags general, so more viewers will see them such as "#beauty," "#makeup," "#lookoftheday." Don't forget to add a hashtag of your brand so users can easily find all your related posts with one comment!

4) **Share video.** Video is the future of visual content, and it's making strides for Instagram. Short clips keep your users engaged and videos have positive responses.

5) **Find, and then build on, your community.** Social media platforms are all about fostering and creating communities of like-minded people. Make sure that you have researched the right groups, accounts, and hashtags that will build your community. Maintaining your share of voice is key in creating a strong digital presence.

6) **Interact.** Without a doubt, one of the most important factors is to interact with your fan base and beyond. Like, share and respond to comments, questions, and feedback. In order to be more than just a brand to your followers, you have to interact like a friend on Instagram

Successful Instagram Brands:

Instagram campaigns require visual stimulation. The key for Instagram will be to engage the customer to post their own picture and tag or hashtag your brand or slogan to further increase visibility. The campaign has to be captivating and creative. It also has to have plenty of room for individual interpretation and unique styling so that the Instagram fans join the campaign.

Starbucks: The social media star Starbucks hosted a great campaign in 2014 with the hashtag #whitecupcontest, that encouraged Starbucks drinkers to paint their cups and post their creations on Twitter and Instagram. The campaign was a hit and resonated with fans across the board while incorporating their product into the images.

https://www.instagram.com/starbucks/

TOMS: TOMS, the philanthropic shoe company which donates a pair of shoes for every pair you buy, went another route and decided not to show their product for their Instagram campaign #withoutshoes in 2015. Instead, they donated a pair of shoes for every person who uploaded an image. It was surely a bold move, but it encouraged users to participate. It also projected their company values. Officially, it resulted in 296,243 shoes being donated.

https://www.instagram.com/toms/

GoPro: Sure GoPro has an edge as a camera device in the field of cool photographs. But as far as Instagram goes, GoPro reigns Supreme. With more than 10 million followers, the brand has curated their feed to feature users photos. From their daily "Photo of the Day" submitted from users, to crazy videos showcasing the breathtaking sights from around the world, GoPro has mastered the art of Instagram. The takeaway: involve your audience. Prizes are offered as rewards. But for most photographers, simply being featured on the highly acclaimed Instagram page would be enough.

https://www.instagram.com/gopro/

Ben & Jerry's: We can't all have the luck of GoPro, whose product seamlessly ties into Instagram. But we can take cues from ice cream dream Ben & Jerry's. As one of the first brands to feature sponsored ads on Instagram, Ben & Jerry's has mastered the art of giving Instagrammers what they love. In terms of content and frequency, the brand has nailed it. With no more than three posts daily, each image is perfectly curated to inspire the viewer on the other end of the phone to get up and buy an ice cream. Furthermore, the brand doesn't shy away from political matters and has proudly supported the "Black Lives Matter" movement, further creating a deeper and more meaningful brand image.

https://www.instagram.com/benandjerrys/

TWITTER

With more than 313 million Twitter users, the demographic are varied. 100 million of these users are active daily. Founded in 2006, Twitter is one of the older social media platforms that still maintains its presence amongst the newcomers. Just like Facebook and Instagram, setting up a Twitter account for your company is easy breezy. Twitter, however, is formatted slightly different than its other social media counterparts, and will, therefore, have a different strategy. Users still have a profile and a feed, which is filled "tweets" from people, brands, and accounts they follow. Tweets are 140-character long messages that are shared to your account. 140 characters is not a lot of room to get your message across, so Twitter features an extra challenge of keeping your messages short, sweet and to the point. Hashtags are still an integral part of Twitter; so don't forget to use them!

Facebook and Instagram focus more on broadcasting your content and your brand, while Twitter is a better-suited platform for communication. With conversations broadcasted to millions of users at a time, Twitter should serve as your direct communication channel to your followers. Twitter chats are highly effective because the users who participate are the ones that are actively engaging on social networks. It's specifically these users that are going to retweet your content and interact with your brand.

Twitter Demographics

The good news for small businesses is that Twitter is ideal for creating brand awareness. 66% of users say that they have discovered a new small or medium-sized business through the platform. Another 79% have retweeted a small business. 94% even plan to make a purchase from a small business that they follow. This is a logical stat since 69% have already made a purchase because of something they saw on Twitter.

Twitter has a powerful international presence. 79% of its account are based outside of the United States, which blends seamlessly given that the platforms offers more than 40 languages. The top three countries outside the US include Brazil, Mexico and Japan, with serious growth prospects in India. Twitter is the perfect platform to reach an international target market, and quickly. Within hours of announcing a new game, PlayStation's tweet had more than 1,800 Retweets and 4,200 likes.

PlayStation @PlayStation 🔵 Follow

Confirmed: Inside is coming to PS4 on August 23.
11:00 PM - 3 Aug 2016
↩ ↻ 1,802 ♥ 4,527

One-third of American teenagers are using Twitter, according to Pew Research study of teen social media usage. Furthermore, high-school aged teens are the most active age demographic on the network, with 42% of online youth aged 15 to 17 on Twitter. The numbers decrease as the age increase, as 32% of Internet users ages 18-29 continue with the network, which holds steady until the age of 50. From then on, only 13% of those aged 50 to 64 uses Twitter.

As for gender, it tends to flip-flop for Twitter. Amongst young teens (13 – 14) boys are more active on Twitter than girls with 23% compared to 19%. But once they hit 15 the statistics change and nearly half of the girls (49%) use Twitter, compared to only 34% of boys. Yet in adulthood, the statistics change again with 25% of men using Twitter compared to 21% of women using Twitter.

An interesting statistic to note is that the divide is greater for adult men who are parents. 10% of moms use Twitter while 27% of dads are on the social media network, with a staggering 7.5 million people identifying themselves as dads in their short Twitter bios. Something about kids has parents researching on Twitter - moms are 67% more likely to research products using Twitter and 45% more likely to make a purchase than women without children.

Main functions of Twitter:

- Sharing information and content

- Direct engagement with Consumers

- Reputation Management

Real Time Marketing Meets Events
Unlike Facebook and Instagram, whose lengthy content has to be carefully crafted, Twitter has the ease of immediate real-time marketing. Users are tweeting their thoughts and opinions in real time, with much less concern towards an aesthetic such as with

Instagram. Don't be afraid to ask your followers' direct questions and add content to your tweets, such as links to your site and videos. Be sure to tweet directly to your audience, with direct wording such as "what do you think about..." or "check this out" instead of just sharing the content without any description.

An example of real-time marketing is what Kit Kat did by responding to the trending topic of iPhone's bending in pockets. A clever caption aided by a strong and simple visual – perfectly and easily gets across the message while humorously staying relevant to users. It's important to relate your brand and content to the events, so get creative and sharpen your wit.

The benefit of real-time marketing is that your brand can be the first when it's necessary. Twitter has a habit of blowing up when something big hits the news, whether it's planned or unplanned. For example, according to Nielsen, for America's biggest sporting event the Superbowl in 2015, more than 65 millions users generated 265 million interactions on Twitter. Make sure your brand has a share in the voice of major events. Such as the Olympics or even real-time events that happen and create a lot of buzzez. This is easily accomplished as Twitter offers a "Trending" review in the sidebar, allowing you to easily see what topics are trending and what users are saying about them. The power of the hashtag is endless.

Repeat Repeat Repeat

Unlike Instagram and Facebook, it's highly recommendable to post several times about the same topic. Not everyone can be logged on always, and unlike its social media counterparts, Twitter users are less likely to check brand profiles. On average, the second post of content will receive as much as 86% engagements as the first time you post it. This is beneficial as it allows you to get creative and vary your content and add details to your messages that may not have fit into the 140-character limitations of the original tweet.

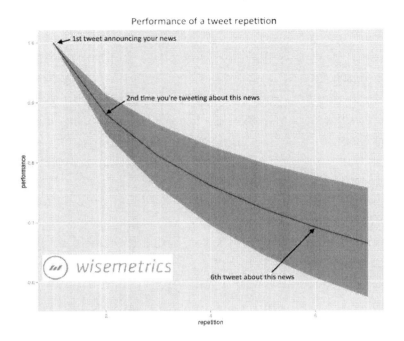

https://audiense.com/wp-content/uploads/2015/02/twiiter_perf_repeat.jpg

SNAPCHAT

The next big thing in digital media has arrived. And you'll only have 10 seconds to see it. Snapchat is taking the digital marketing world by storm and has changed the way brands interact with their customer base. Compared to the top dogs like Facebook and Instagram, Snapchat is still a 'relatively' small niche audience. But that doesn't mean you should rule it out for your next digital media strategy. The app is one of the newer ones on the market. It launched in 2011 and Snapchat marketing really took off in 2015. And Snapchat is only growing, with eMarketer forecasts estimating that by the end of 2016 there will be more users on Snapchat than Twitter or Pinterest. The key challenge with Snapchat is figuring out a way to promote without giving direct promotional ads.

The video-centric social media app has 100 million active users. They spend on average 25 to 30 minutes on the app daily and watch a total of 8 billion videos per day. This is tied neck-to-neck with Facebook. Even though the later has more than 1 billion daily active users. In fact, users are so active that 65% upload Snaps.

Sample of Snapchat Screen for personal users
https://www.pinterest.com/ISeeBliss/snapchat-wechat-whatsapp-tips/

Snapchat is also unique in that it's vertical. While Instagram and Facebook have visuals optimized for square shots, i.e. 4 x 4, Snapchat has embraced the smartphone shape. It captures video in the full vertical format.

How It Works

Snapchat is unique to other social media; the content uploaded by users disappears after 24 hours. Users can direct message each other pictures or video clips that are up to 10-seconds long, or they can upload the content to their Story, which their followers can view. After one day, the content will disappear for good, unless you are able to take a screenshot of the image. In the age where nothing can be removed from the Internet, it seems that vanishing images and ten-second clips resonate with the masses.

Demographics

Snapchat is a gold mine for the Millennial demographic, specifically 18 to 34 year-olds. It's a relatively young niche, with 60% of users under the age of 25 and only 12% of users are between 34 and 54. While that may seem overwhelmingly young, it's important to keep in mind that the youngsters are usually the one setting the trends. Reportedly, half of all new users registering on Snapchat are over 25. That is a staggering number since as early as 2013 only 5% of Snapchat users were over 25. Snapchat still has the cool factor as parents (and even grandparents) haven't yet discovered the app – creating more interest in the app than the older social networks such as Facebook.

As is commonly seen trending for visual based apps and platforms, women seem to have the upper hand in users. 42% of women ages 18-29 have Snapchat accounts, compared to only 31% of male respondents in a Harvard study from Fall 2015.

Understanding the Culture of Snapchat

Snapchat is the most real time of all the apps. It records and captures real-time content by users and has to be uploaded instantly in order to be viewed. Snapchat also lets users get creative by letting them draw and add "Stickers" over their images and video, which often results in funny captions and colorful images. Snapchat is arguably the most fun platform out of the bunch and users expect brands to play into that. Your brand should not take itself too seriously in order to have a successful Snapchat account. And most definitely don't push your product. You want the videos to feel natural, so keep the name-dropping and product placement low. Be sure to use Snapchat's set up to your advantage and tell a story.

You should offer a "behind-the-scenes" look into how your brand and your team act and work together. Snapchat is the ultimate tool to allow you to humanize your brand. Content should be real, genuine and most of all entertaining. For example, if you are hosting an event, be sure to capture the moment before the event in order to draw an audience to your event. Take videos while preparing or a funny selfie right before you get up on stage. You don't necessarily need to plan out what you post and have more creative agency. You can create content in the moment and feed off of what is happening in real time. By offering a behind the scenes look at your brand and the people that make the brand, you can easily create a certain amount of anticipation for an event or product launch.

Advertising on Snapchat

Ads are still new to Snapchat, and therefore far and few between and reserved for the big spenders. But they do promising!

One way that brands can advertise on Snapchat is through uniquely designed "filters" which can be applied to photos or videos that users send. The unbeatable benefit of Snapchat filters is that they take up the whole screen. So users won't be able to ignore the message as easily as they would on other platforms. In that way, the message are not an afterthought, but rather the main event.

One successful campaign on Snapchat was (RED)'s Global one-day-only Geofilter commemorating World AIDS Day. For each Geofilter applied, the Bill and Melinda Gates Foundation donated $3 to (RED) for the fight against AIDS internationally. The campaign was a huge success and reached 14 million Snapchatters and had a total of 76 million views worldwide. A staggering number considering there are only 24 hours for content to be viewed.

PINTEREST

As the self-titled "catalogue" of ideas, Pinterest is leading the Internet with inspiration boards ranging from bridal preparations to travel. From inspirational quotes to recipes, from cats to vintage cars. It allows users to "pin" ideas to a "board" thereby sharing content from brand profiles and other users. Users can set up boards for a variety of things. But boards are heavily visual and rely on photographs to share content. It's practical and easy to use as well as highly organized. Pinterest is a hit as it allows for portable and easy to use images to serve as inspiration. Brides-to-be can ditch the heavy three ring binders and opt to prepare everything digitally. Likewise aspiring cooks can collects hundreds and thousands of recipes without printing a single page and with the aid of perfectly curated images.

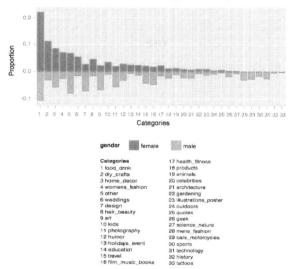

https://blog.kissmetrics.com/wp-
content/uploads/2015/01/pinterest_categories.jpg

The social aspect comes from the nature liking, repining or working together on Boards. Users can also follow Boards they find especially interesting and keep up to date on their updates. Furthermore, you can share pins on other platforms including Facebook, Twitter or LinkedIn.

The Power of the Keywords

On the site itself, Pinterest recommends that each pin has 20 – 30 keywords that would optimize it for search tools. Don't be afraid to get specific, such as "healthy dinner for two" if you are creating a post about clean eating. It's the best way to make sure that new users can find you and that you will reach a wider target market. Keep the descriptions short and sweet, at around 100 – 300 words. Make sure that you are describing all of the necessary components, but that your pictures are telling the story. Pinterest has had a huge hit with visual instructional, i.e. how to's that are graphic and visual in nature. Furthermore, if you are selling a product – be sure to include a direct link to the online shop as well as a price point. Pinterest is a natural and easy first stop to an online shopping spree, so be sure that your brand is amongst the first that they see.

In partnership with influencer @Erin
Freedman - With the weather
warming up, it's time to grow! This
is a fun and easy way to go about it,
too. Plus, growing your own food is
the best! To start, gather jars, cups
or tiny pots for your seeds. Fill each
3/4 of the way full with Nature's

YouTube

Pexel: https://www.pexels.com/photo/mokup-smartphone-technology-phone-34407/

There is a lot of misconception about YouTube as a social media platform. Because of the ease with which users can update and create their own content, it often seems like less of a social media network and more of a personal page. But just because you can use Facebook, Twitter and the like to promote your video, doesn't mean that YouTube isn't a viable social media platform. In fact, YouTube can be seen as the heart of the social media platforms as its content is widely distributed throughout the other platforms. In fact, 400 tweets per minute contain a YouTube link, and YouTube's search bar is the second only after Google.

YouTube has the benefit of having one of the most engaged audiences out of the social media platforms. With tweets flooding Twitter news feeds, and posts cluttering Facebook feeds, it's harder than ever to reach followers on platforms. However, 85% of YouTube subscribers consider themselves "regular" YouTube users.

It's recommended that if you do pursue creating a YouTube channel that you have a professional team of producers and creators as the content uploaded should maintain a high standard. However, a lot of big Youtubers have started with just their mobile phone and a personality. Now, video content and a strong YouTube presence can be significantly harder to establish than say Twitter, Facebook or Instagram. But if video content were right for your brand, it would be well worth the extra step.

As YouTube is free to set up (and easy - all you need is your Gmail address, and you're set), the company makes its massive profits from ads. While they are reserved for those top budget players, YouTube still has certain issues with the ads as they are considered a form of interruption messaging, i.e. not organic content that is so highly favored on other social media platforms. Essentially, the paid ads are disrupting viewers from what they are doing on the site. And with the ease of the "Skip Now" button, the ads have a high chance of not being viewed if they are not properly targeted.

Make your profile follow other guidelines for social media, i.e. interacting with followers and comments and sharing your link on all platforms.

The importance of keywords
Youtube is a search engine that is owned by Google. So remember to add keywords to the title and description of your Youtube videos. I recommend adding the keyword once in the title and around three times in the description. Make sure to make it natural – so write three paragraphs and spread out your keyword. You can also "tag" your video with different keywords.

Here is an example of a video that is optimized for the keyword phrase "How to create a blog":

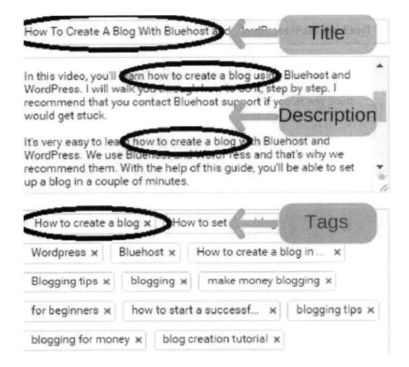

LINKEDIN

Unlike the other social media platforms, LinkedIn isn't for fun and games. The platform is used to connect business professionals across fields and countries. While you can still have fun with the posts, remember that LinkedIn is a professional site, so keep up with the proper decorum and post related content. LinkedIn is a platform where you can post more regarding your business and its progress than on other social media platforms. People on Facebook and Instagram want to be entertained and bedazzled, but people on LinkedIn want to be informed and educated. LinkedIn is the optimized platform for B2B Marketing, (business-to-business marketing).

Users can follow your company, so make sure that there is a visible "Share" button on all of the content you post on your profile. Set up and maintain a group on LinkedIn. The people who follow and engage in your group will be your most loyal followers, so be sure to keep posting content and engaging in dialogue with users. There is a lot less dialogue happening on profiles on LinkedIn than other pages, so it's incredibly important to create a Group and stay active in varying Groups to promote your business. Groups allow you to meet and interact with people in the same industry, so don't be shy and ask questions that keep conversations flowing. It will be an essential role in establishing yourself as a leader in your field.

LinkedIn is a great place for advocated and even your employees to promote your content, brand, products and services. The platform was designed specifically for businesses and employees in mind. It offers a prime opportunity to show the world what you have to offer them, without the need of entertaining that other social media platforms pose.

To gain followers on LinkedIn, the best strategy is to be directly engaged. Start discussions, ask questions and respond to comments. The more interactive you are, the bigger and bolder your presence will be, thereby creating a larger following.

GOOGLE PLUS

With Google's fourth endeavor into social media, Google Plus seems to be the place to be for your all around social media presence. Several features streamline Google Plus to be the ideal platform to connect your business with relevant people. With as little as your Gmail account you will be able to create a profile, which will automatically connect you to your contacts, which you can sort by Circles i.e. family, travel friends from Bali, co-workers, etc. Circles act like filters in the way that you can share content with only certain Groups. People within a group will be notified when you share with them, but other won't know.

Unlike Facebook, which encourages users to connect with people you already know – Google Plus has taken a different approach to connecting with people. It allows you to easily connects people who have similar interests, passions, hobbies and careers. Google Plus allows you to bring your brand closer to new potential customers. Google Plus also has the added benefit of increasing your search engine views as everything you share on the platform is indexed by Google and therefore positively influences your search engine results.

Google Plus offers the streamlined benefits of connecting Google, Gmail, Google Maps, and YouTube on communities and hangouts, which are the primary spots where users interact on the platform. You can create a community that's relevant and important for potential new customers and loyal followers alike. Just like the chocolate connoisseur Cadbury did, with a community of more than 76 thousand members. Communities allow you to create engagement, but also position your brand in a social network as well as increase your ranking of Google's search engine, further establishing your brand presence as a leader in your field.

Unlike other social networks, there is more control over what users can see on Google Plus. There is also more room to write lengthy posts with the ability to easily connect with your audience, which isn't the case on other platforms like Twitter and Instagram.

TUMBLR

Tumblr can be seen as Pinterest's less organized cousin. The microblogging site launched in 2007 has garnered significant attention. But it is not a leading social media platform for all markets. However, with more than 420 million users, there is surely a niche market or two to target with Tumblr.

It works similarly to Pinterest in the way that users can create profiles and upload or share posts that they enjoy. For the most part, these posts are highly visual and usually photographs, although video posts are not uncommon. But pictures take the cake with 78% of content on Tumblr, which is also the most liked and shared content.

tumblr. Post Types Breakdown

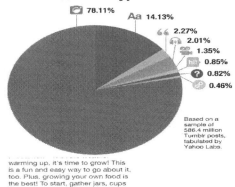

78.11% Aa 14.13%
2.27%
2.01%
1.35%
0.85%
0.82%
0.46%

Based on a sample of 586.4 million Tumblr posts, tabulated by Yahoo Labs.

warming up, it's time to grow! This is a fun and easy way to go about it, too. Plus, growing your own food is the best! To start, gather jars, cups or tiny pots for your seeds. Fill each 3/4 of the way full with Nature's

http://www.socialmediatoday.com/social-networks/complete-starters-guide-tumblr-marketing

Bear in mind that a whopping 39% of Tumblr users are under the age of 25, so it is definitely geared toward a younger market.

Reaching older target markets would not be effectively accomplished on Tumblr.

The benefit of Tumblr is that you can format the page how you want. With traditional social media such as Facebook and Instagram, you are restricted to the format. Essentially you have one set up, and you need to fill the spaces with your content. Tumblr, however, operates similarly to the blog creating website Wordpress and allows you to customize your page with different themes. This is beneficial because you can tailor your Tumblr to perfectly suit your needs. Tumblr, therefore, functions somewhere in between a Pinterest account (due to the overwhelming visual content and inspiration based feed) and a personal blog. Because of the blog format, Tumblr has the benefit that when people share your content, it directly links back to your profile, known as do-follow links, which are highly beneficial to your site in terms of SEO.

All in all, Tumblr could serve to benefit your brand by further providing a source of information and inspiration to your followers. You can showcase your products or post inspirational material. You have the benefit of tailoring the site to your liking, thereby creating a pin board that perfectly represents you. But be wary – a Tumblr shouldn't take the pace of an actual website.

BLURRING THE LINES OF SOCIAL MEDIA PLATFORMS

The aforementioned social media platforms all serve their own distinct purpose. Yet as the digital world evolves and competition increases, it is important to keep in mind the ever-blurring lines of social media, and how those could impact your business and your social media marketing strategy. For example, Facebook has its own Messenger app, which blurs the line social media network and messaging. Instagram has recently adopted a new feature that allows videos to be posted for a temporary time before they vanish. Sure does sound an awful lot like Snapchat, doesn't it? As social media networks develop and grow, they learn from each other. It's important to take note of that growth and development and stay on top of the game.

PART 3

GOING VIRAL

CHAPTER 17

WHAT DOES IT MEAN TO GO VIRAL

Before we discuss how to go viral, let's dissect what it actually means for content to go viral on the Internet. More often than not, the content that goes viral is an Internet meme – something that spreads virally from one person to another via social media or email. A meme can be anything, but it's usually a short funny clip or a relatable photo with some texts.

Viral images and videos don't follow a certain formula. The common theme is that viral videos or photos are interesting, easy to share and relatable. The word 'viral' is relatively new and didn't come about until the hilarious clip of "David after Dentist" in 2009. In that clip, a dad filmed his son after a trip to the dentist and a healthy dose of anesthesia, which resulted in a hilarious video of the boy. This unplanned video has amassed more than 133 million views on YouTube and was shared millions of times.

And there's a profit to be made from these viral stars that start out from nothing. Brands have capitalized on the overnight stardom and have recently been incorporating viral stars as their leads in ads in place of celebrities. And the species doesn't matter. Even lovable dogs such as Tony with the under bite go on to "write" books and travel across the country on book tours.

Unfortunately, there is no formula or trick to content going viral. It is precisely that unexpected fervor and the unplanned, in-the-moment captures which captivate an audience and inspire people to share the content millions of times.

It is noteworthy, however, to examine videos and campaigns that went viral seemingly overnight and draw insights from why they went viral.

CHAPTER 18

CASE STUDIES OF VIRAL CONTENT

KONY 2012

http://theweek.com/articles/476909/rise-fall-kony-2012-campaign-timeline

In the relatively early days of social media, KONY took the internet by storm. The 30-minute documentary about Ugandan rebel leader Joseph Kony was viewed more than 100 million times within less than one week. The campaign – which advocates for the arrest and persecution of Joseph Kony by the International Criminal Court – used an online video to spread its message and raise the profile of Kony on an international scale. Within a few days, KONY merchandise from the campaign was visible on your Millennial across the world, sporting their canvas totes and wristbands. The video – relatively long considering other success stories behind viral content – was moving and beautifully executed. One of the most interesting aspects of the campaign is the sheer volume of conversations it sparked globally. The number of articles, blog posts, news reports, verbal debates and social media conversations about Kony has turned the audience's attention to the issue. The campaign wasn't without scrutiny, as its legitimacy was often challenged. But it succeeded in drawing attention to an international issue.

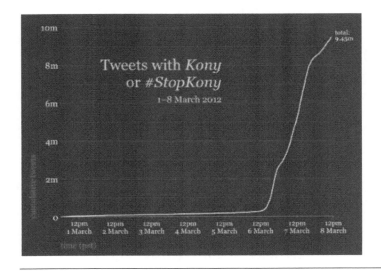

Key Takeaways

- ✓ **Directly involve the viewer**. The video opens with Invisible Children Founder Jason Russell's footage of his son's birth. This directly reminds the viewer with a voiceover that the child represents all of us; "He didn't choose where or when he was born, but because he's here, he matters." The directness of the opening line enthralls viewers and involves them on an emotional level.

- ✓ **Have a clear message**. The slogans for the campaign were irrefutable, clear and loud. "Make Kony famous" and "Stop at nothing" are easily understood messages that get the message across without any frills.

- ✓ **Simplify Your Call to Action**. There was a clear end goal for the viral video and campaign, and the call to actions were simple: "Wear the Bracelet," "Sign the Pledge," and "Share the Film." Participation in the campaign was simplified and snackable so that all Internet users could easily sign the pledge and share the content – thereby increasing the visibility of the campaign.

- ✓ **Create a movement beyond the Internet.** The campaign was successful because the message resonated with people beyond the world of social media. The wearable bracelets and shirts increased revenue and sales for Invisible Children. But it also perpetuated the message on the streets. There was a tangible message for the KONY campaign that was undeniable in their success.

It should be noted that KONY did not come from scratch. The video was extremely well produced and of the highest quality. The parent organization Invisible Children, already had a tremendous following on social media. This allowed the campaign to create a spring-off board from where they could start. Nonetheless, the campaign blew up tremendously in an incredibly short amount of time.

ALS ICE BUCKET CHALLENGE 2014

http://marketingland.com/als-ice-bucket-challenge-viral-success-cause-96463

In what can only be considered the world's longest chain letter ever, the ALS ice bucket challenge took the Internet by storm in 2014. The concept was simple enough so that anyone could join – but hilarious enough to have people watching over and over again. In what seemed like an endless watching cycle that lasted months, people would pour a bucket of ice water on themselves and nominate three others to do the same. If they didn't pour ice water on themselves, they would have to donate to the charitable company, raising awareness and funds for ALS.

The campaign was a huge hit, with celebrities such as Facebook founder Mark Zuckerberg, Oprah, LeBron James, Bill Gates, Steven Spielberg joining in on the challenge. For the month of August, it was impossible to log onto your Facebook feed without seeing a friend tag another friend about the ALS Ice Bucket challenge. Sure, the videos weren't educational – in fact, the debilitating side effects of ALS were completely disregarded. But in the end, the viral campaign raised $115 million dollars, which is an astounding number for an organization that in the previous year had only billed $23 million.

Key Takeaways

✓ **Play up the right emotions.** ALS is no laughing matter, but the campaign took a turn for the humorous. It can be surely assumed that the campaign wouldn't have been a success if it focused on negative emotional responses, such as sadness. The campaign had a feel-good momentum to it that didn't take itself too seriously. "Schadenfreude", the concept that people get a certain sense of pleasure from seeing others suffer, is at play here. It just is pretty hilarious watching friends and celebs get doused in freezing cold water.

✓ **Engage the Audience.** The ALS Ice Bucket Challenge went viral because it was so easily shareable. The entire concept of the campaign was to involve people, and then share their videos. It's sheer digital marketing genius as it ensures that there is always new content being shared.

✓ **Get in on the celebrity endorsements.** While the ALS campaign was doing alright, it really skyrocketed as soon as celebrities join in on the fun. With millions of Twitter followers and Instagram loyals, getting celebrities to join the bandwagon is key for making content go viral. With just one

Tweet, they can spread a message to millions of followers. And that power is indisputable in raising awareness for a campaign. Sure, the celebs didn't get all of their followers to join in on the action for the ALS campaign. But they did spread the message.

HARLEM SHAKE

https://theamericangenius.com/business-marketing/harlem-shake-videos-by-businesses-please-die/

The viral and tremendous popularity of the Harlem Shake video depicts the emergent behavior of viral videos; accidental, ad hoc and uncoordinated. On February 2 in Caloundra, Australia several friends released a 36-second clip of themselves dancing to Baauer's then hit single "Harlem Shake." The video was silly enough. It had one star dancing alone for the first half. And after the bass drop, he was getting joined by several of his friends, and then they all danced disjointedly. The next day an American teen in America made her own version of the video with her friends, and a few days later several hundred thousand viewers had seen both clips on YouTube. Within days, the videos went viral, with friends, school teams and companies making their own versions of the funny dance. And the stakes were high. University of Georgia's Olympic winning swim team even filmed their Harlem Shake under the water.

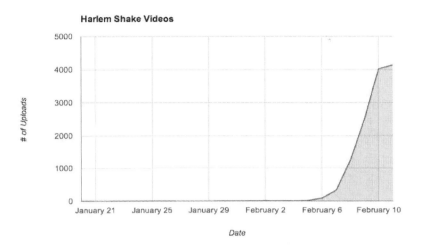

So what gives? The relatively unpopular song at the time wasn't the inspiration for all the videos. Rather it was the status with which people could easily create and remake the video into a work of their own. So much so that within days 44,000 new videos had been uploaded and all collectively watched. The original video has amassed more than 2.6 million views on YouTube, which isn't even the most watched video. Articles on Huffington Post and Buzzfeed spread like wildfire, and before the break of dawn, the Harlem Shake had spread to the masses.

While all these videos are user-generated, brands were quick to react and created their own Harlem Shake videos. Pepsi, the Daily Show, Maker Studios and AOL are amongst the several brands that were able to create their own videos and be part of the noise. By joining in to what their customers are doing, the brands became more relatable and their content shared. It may not have led to direct sales, but building brand awareness should not be discarded as something small.

Key Takeaways

- ✓ **Stay on top of the trends.** Viral sensations happen overnight – literally. It's important to be one of the first to react because the heat with which these viral videos come to life and implode is often just as quickly extinguished. Timing is vital and catching onto a trend as a brand before it becomes old news is key in getting your message spread first.

- ✓ **Create content that has potential to be reinvented.** What made Harlem Shake so great was the creative groups of friends, coworkers or families who could showcase their quirky characteristics in the video. It wasn't one video that went viral; it was a movement that allowed space for new creation and new content. Such trends should be noted as ultimately this is what the Internet was meant to do – connect people.

ALWAYS LIKE A GIRL

https://www.theodysseyonline.com/why-the-like-girl-campaign-matters

It's pretty difficult to get people to talk about periods. They're unwelcome, painful and frankly; most women don't want to spend much time thinking about purchasing products like tampons. So Always was tasked with the difficulty of raising brand awareness around the uncomfortable topic of periods. Leo Burnette was the ad agency responsible for the campaign that eventually went viral. They took a cue from previous viral hits and noted that focusing on social issues usually gets people going. Digging deeper into gender stereotypes, the team realized that issues in young women's confidence plummeted during their teenage years. The video which they went on to create was just over 3 minutes long and juxtaposed adults and young girls reacting to the phrase "Like a Girl." It was a moving and shocking video as all of the adults acted as one would expect: they ran like they were in pain, threw an imaginary ball like their arm was about to fall off and didn't have much power behind their punches. The girls on the other hand – yet untouched by the insecurities of puberty and societal expectations of women – ran as fast as they could when they heard "run like a girl" and punched through the air with all their might when told to "hit like a girl." The contrast was jarring and moving, and the Internet took notice.

With over 67 million views on YouTube, the campaign was a huge hit. It resonated with millions of women across the globe, and a 30-second spot was even featured at the Superbowl, which usually only airs commercials for men such as Axe Body Spray or beer adverts. The campaign went on to have tremendous success, winning award after award, but more than just winning awards at prestigious Advertising events, the campaign resonated with consumers across the globe.

Key Takeaways

- ✓ **Support a Social cause.** Brands need to align themselves with their consumers more than on a practical level. People are more likely to support brands that share the same values. Addressing a bigger issue and aligning yourself with a movement creates a persona behind your brand. Supporting the empowerment of women clearly aligns Always with a social cause and inevitably will increase support from a broad range of people.

- ✓ **Be Bold.** Take a stance. Nothing has gone viral that didn't break the norm. In order to be worthy of being shared hundreds and thousands and millions of times, your content needs to break barriers and be utterly unique. Before anything, it has to be share-worthy. In order to be worthy of a coveted spot in millions of newsfeeds, the content needs to be daring, provocative and bold. Always took a chance by addressing a sensitive social issue, but it struck a chord with men and women alike.

✓ **Remember that Creating Brand Awareness Doesn't Always Require the Presence of the Product.** The campaign was a success, given that it was viewed 90 million times within the first week of release. But it is noteworthy that Always made a campaign that didn't feature its signature products, such as pads and tampons. You don't need to promote your brand using only your product or services. Consumers expect more from brands in the 21st century, so go above and beyond what you offer them and show them who you are.

✓ **Create a Hashtag.** The campaign was a hit on its own accord, but the clever, and easily understood hashtag helped propel the video to social media success. Within the first three months, there were over 117,000 tweets with the hashtag #LikeAGirl. The campaign was easily understood with the hashtag and was therefore easily shareable on a variety of social media networks

PART 4

CREATING A SOCIAL MEDIA STRATEGY

CHAPTER 19

HOW TO CREATE YOUR SOCIAL MEDIA STRATEGY

With all the basic know-how covered, it's time to create your Social Media Marketing Strategy. While it may seem like an overwhelming task for the newcomer, I'll break it down for you as simply as possible.

1. Create social media objectives and goals

2. Conduct a social media audit

3. Create (or improve) your social media accounts

4. Get inspired

5. Create a content plan and an editorial calendar

6. Evaluate your social media plan

Step 1: Create social media objectives and goals

Before you can consider the scope of your social media marketing strategy, you have to set clear and attainable objectives. These goals should be easily aligned with your overall marketing strategy and fit within your budget.

An easy-to-use framework is SMART. Each objective should be:

Specific

Measurable

Attainable

Relevant

Time-bound

An example of a SMART objective is as follows: "For Facebook this week, we will post photos that communicate our company culture. We will post three photos this week and one video. The target for each item posted is 100 likes and 10 comments.

It's important to make sure that your goals are measurable, in whichever way is necessary and most useful for your company.

In order to address your objectives, you will need to address your problems, or the aspects of your business that need improving. Is your overall brand awareness low? Is there room for improvement for your customer service? Are you doing everything you can to retain your old customers while attracting new ones?

Step 2: Conduct a social media audit

Once you decide what your objectives are for your social media campaign, it's time to figure out your target market and what social media they frequent the most. It's important to decipher key demographics including age, gender, occupation, disposable income, interests, likes, dislikes, and motivations. Creating a sample user profile will help you better narrow down your target market.

Keeping in mind questions that you need to ask about your ideal brand persona, such as:

- where they get their information from

- where they shop online

- where do they consume their digital content

- what channels do they frequently / not frequently use

After you have narrowed down who your target market is, research your competition. It is important to be aware of the digital presence of your competitors and what channels they are using to get to their target market. Keep note of their engagement and what content seems to be performing better. As you most likely won't have access to their information – just doing a quick scan on their sites will do.

Step 3: Create Your Social Media Accounts (or update them)

Based on the information thus far, you can set up your accounts according to your need. Be sure to have a running theme across your platforms. Your profile pictures should be the same and the descriptions not too varied. Keep the descriptions short, sweet and to the point without overwhelming newcomers. Be sure to clearly state what business you are in. Keep in mind that your images should be of the highest quality, and the overall look of your social media pages should be clean.

Step 4: Get Inspired

Sure, your budget may not rival that of international giants such as Nike and Coca-Cola. But don't be shy in getting inspired by their social media tactics. Do your research and keep tabs on the big brand names as well as the smaller brands who are making waves with their social media presence. Keeping up with the latest trends is key. For example, if you notice that video posts are getting higher traction and more following, you should consider incorporating video into your social media strategy.

Content is vital to your social media strategy, for your social media is null and void without strong content – either in the form of blogs, visual aids, or videos. Keep in mind that your calendar should be a wide spanning calendar. Have fun with it. For example, if National Smile Day is coming up in the next month, be sure to creatively incorporate that into your feeds – either by having users upload photos of themselves smiling with your product or uploading a silly and lighthearted photo of your team leader. Keep big events and dates in your calendar. More than just keeping track of what's already planned, keep up with the new so your brand can stay ahead of the curve and relate your brand and content to the news.

Step 5: Create a content plan and an editorial calendar

Content is vital to your social media strategy, for your social media is null and void without strong content – either in the form of blogs, visual aids, or videos. Keep in mind that your calendar should be a wide spanning calendar. Have fun with it. For example, if National Smile Day is coming up in the next month, be sure to creatively incorporate that into your feeds – either by having users upload photos of themselves smiling with your product or uploading a silly and lighthearted photo of your team leader. Keep big events and dates in your calendar. More than just keeping track of what's already planned, keep up with the new so your brand can stay ahead of the curve and relate your brand and content to the news.

Step 6: Evaluate Your Social Media Plan

Based on the parameters you have chosen in step 1, it is important to frequently touch base with your social media platform and see how they are performing. There are different metrics for tracking success on social media so make sure to choose the right ones for you. The world of social media is fast moving, so don't get hung up on failures, or successes. Content may go viral one week, but can just as quickly be irrelevant the following week. If a strategy didn't work as planned, learn from the mistakes you made and adapt for the future.

TIPS FOR YOUR SOCIAL MEDIA STRATEGY

- **Make sharing as easy as possible.** The end goal of posting content is that it should be seen and engaged by with as many people as possible. Therefore, it is of utmost importance that each piece of content you share is easily shareable no matter what platform you are using. Make sure that your blog or website has easily visible plug-ins and sharing options for all of the different social media platforms. SumoMe is one example of such a plugin.

- **Keep it visual.** The easiest way to grab the attention of users that are inundated with content on their feeds is to feature an accompanying image or video with text. Visual aids stimulate and encourage engagement and content featuring visual aid is more likely to be seen than content without.

- **Don't underestimate the power of the headline.** With so much content clogging our feeds, headlines are unforgiving and often times the first piece of content that viewers will see on their site. Attention spans are continuing to dwindle and you will need catchy headlines to attract readers to your links and content. Keep in mind that audiences favor snackabiltilty, so your headline should be brief and informative and easily shareable. It shouldn't reveal too much about what you are posting, because after all you do want the audience to click through on the link.

- **Listen up.** Digital marketers need to know how to listen and catch wind of the latest buzz on the Internet. Don't be afraid to use social analytical tools and listening software to see what is trending on social media. You can gain valuable insight from the data that you gather.

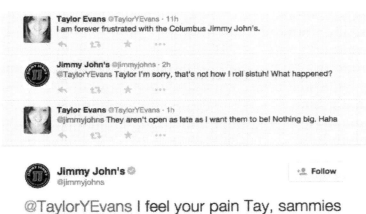

CONCLUSION

It may seem as if marketing has become more complex. And perhaps it is more difficult, but there are also more opportunities now than ever before. By following the strategies outlined in this book, you'll be able to prosper in this new game called social media marketing. I recommend that you revisit this book several times to get the most out of it. But just to do a quick recap, here are a few of the things that were covered throughout the book:

In part 1 of this book, you received a general overview of social media. Just some of the topics that were discussed involved the decline of traditional media as well as the rise of the smartphone. You also learned how to measure success & social media metrics along with the link between Social Media Marketing (SMM) and Search Engine Optimization (SEO).

Part 2 of the book covered social media platforms. There, we started off with some general tips for social media, followed with some Do's and Don'ts. We then dived into the rise of social influencers and how they can benefit your brand. We discussed the importance of organic content, but also gave you information about options for paid traffic. Furthermore, you discovered how it can benefit your brand to engage itself in a cause (cause related marketing). Lastly, we dived deeper into each individual platform. There, you got information about the demographics which can help you to decide whether or not it's the right platform for your brand. You learned from the best brands, got lot of different methods to promote your company, along with information on how to use keywords to get more exposure.

In part 3 we analyzed viral content. You now know what's behind viral content and hopefully you'll be able to create a viral campaign of your own.

Last but not least, we went into part 4 where you received practical information on how to create your own social media marketing strategy.

Social media is the wild, wild west of marketing. With the ever-changing platforms and networks, anything is possible. Make your presence known and get on the networks, or else you'll fall behind. Stay creative and most of all have fun with it. Happy Marketing!

Want Free Help With Setting Up An Email List?

FREE Video Course Reveals...

"How To Create An Email List To Increase Recurring Visitors And Sales (Step By Step Tutorial)"

- The Basics of Building An Email List
- Ways Of Creating a Giveaway That Your Visitors Will Love
- How To Create An Awesome Squeeze page/Landing page With LeadPages
- Technical things like Integrating your LeadPages account with your AWeber account
- How To Create an Opt-in (Leadbox) That You Can Place Somewhere On Your Website
- How To Promote your Squeeze Page and Leadbox and Get Thousands of Emails
- Much more!

Get Access to this NEW Video Course + Manual For FREE Now Before The Gate Closes...

To access this free video course and manual, go to:

www.freedombasedbusinesses.com/email-course

Follow our blog

Follow Freedombasedbusinesses.com to get more help with online marketing.

Here are some articles that we think you might like:

SEO for Beginners: How To Improve Your Search Engine Ranking
http://www.freedombasedbusinesses.com/seo-for-beginners/

How To Find Keywords and Optimize Your Blog Posts For The Search Engine
http://www.freedombasedbusinesses.com/how-to-find-keywords/

How to Create a Blog with WordPress and Bluehost (Free Step By Step Guide)
http://www.freedombasedbusinesses.com/how-to-create-a-blog/

33 Ways to Immediately Improve Your Blogging
http://www.freedombasedbusinesses.com/improve-blogging/

How To Make Money From Blogging
http://www.freedombasedbusinesses.com/how-to-make-money-from-blogging/

Top 3 Reasons Why Most Bloggers Don't Make Money From Their Blog

http://www.freedombasedbusinesses.com/bloggers/

Top 3 Reasons to Why You Should Build An Email List Today

http://www.freedombasedbusinesses.com/build-an-email-list/

The One Thing That No One Can Take Away From Your Online Business

http://www.freedombasedbusinesses.com/the-one-propery/

AWeber Review: What Is AWeber Communications and Why Did We Choose Them For Email Marketing?

http://www.freedombasedbusinesses.com/aweber-review/

9 Reasons Why So Many Entrepreneurs Fail

http://www.freedombasedbusinesses.com/reason-entrepreneurs-fail/

A Complete Guide To Budgeting Your Personal Finances

http://www.freedombasedbusinesses.com/budgeting-guide/

One Important Law Regarding Multiple Streams of Income

http://www.freedombasedbusinesses.com/multiple-streams-of-income/

100 Ways to Make Extra Money

http://www.freedombasedbusinesses.com/100-ways-to-make-extra-money/

NOTES

[1] Brandwatch Blog; 96 Amazing Social Media Statistics and Facts for 2016; Kit Smith, March 7 2016; https://www.brandwatch.com/2016/03/96-amazing-social-media-statistics-and-facts-for-2016/

[2.] Pew Research Center; Data Trend; Updated 2016 http://www.pewinternet.org/data-trend/social-media/social-media-use-by-age-group/

[3] Smart Insights; Mobile Marketing Statistics Compilation; April 27 2016 http://www.smartinsights.com/mobile-marketing/mobile-marketing-analytics/mobile-marketing-statistics/

[4] Mavrck; Most Influential Brands of 2016; Caroline Burke; February 23, 2016 http://www.mavrck.co/the-most-influential-brands-on-facebook-in-2016/

[5] http://expandedramblings.com/index.php/march-2013-by-the-numbers-a-few-amazing-twitter-stats/3/

[6] Hootsuit, August 2016 https://blog.hootsuite.com/twitter-demographics/

[7] "Should You Repeat Your Tweets?" Oct 24 2014; Wiselytics; http://www.wiselytics.com/blog/should-you-repeat-your-tweets-facts-and-figures-from-1m-tweets/

[8] Harvard Polls Fall 2015, http://iop.harvard.edu/survey/details/harvard-iop-fall-2015-poll